The Essential Wedding Planning Guide

Cost Saving Tips, Checklists, Vendor Interview Questions, Budget Worksheet and More

Tiara Ward Cable

The Essential Wedding Planning Guide

ISBN 1449558011

Dedication

This book is dedicated to my husband Brandon and my mother Sheila for their ongoing support and encouragement that help me reach my goals of attaining a successful event planning business. Also, to my grandmother Clara who is my mentor in life and business.

Contents

Chapter One

CHECKLIST:

The checklist is an important tool to have for the bride and groom to help keep you on schedule with the wedding planning process. It is very easy to fall behind and to become overwhelmed with details toward your wedding date. Use the following checklist to keep organized as certain deadlines come about.

THE BRIDES CHECKLIST:

12 Months Before the wedding

☐ Select a wedding consultant to help you avoid wasting time or money
☐ Confirm ceremony date, time, and site with officiant
☐ Set a preliminary budget
☐ Select attendants
☐ Reserve the reception site
☐ Select and book caterers, photographers, videographers, florists, musicians, and other service providers
☐ Begin compiling guest list
☐ Select wedding dress, headpiece, and bridesmaid's dresses
☐ Start thinking about your honeymoon

9 Months Before

- ☐ Attend premarital classes
- ☐ Choose and order your dress accessories
- ☐ Register for china, gifts, etc.
- ☐ Shop for a new home

6 Months Before

- ☐ Place deposits and sign contracts for wedding services
- ☐ Choose bridesmaid's dresses and accessories
- ☐ Choose flower girl's dress
- ☐ Make sure your visas and passports are up to date, if you're traveling
- ☐ Complete honeymoon plans with groom
- ☐ Discuss rehearsal dinner with groom
- ☐ Avoid skin problems early by making an appointment with a licensed esthetician

4 Months Before

- ☐ Verify that the wedding gown, bridesmaid's dresses, and flower girl dress have been ordered
- ☐ Make sure addresses for guest list are up to date
- ☐ Order invitations, announcements, and any other personal stationary
- ☐ Choose and order formal wear for groom and attendants
- ☐ Make sure all out-of-town male attendants have submitted their measurements to your formal wear provider
- ☐ Verify that both mothers have selected and ordered either dresses
- ☐ Investigate requirements for medical test and other records for your marriage license
- ☐ Design a map to direct guests to the ceremony and reception sites
- ☐ Complete registering
- ☐ Shop for trousseau

2 Months before

- ☐ Schedule final fitting
- ☐ Finalize bridal registry
- ☐ Confirm ceremony details with your officiant
- ☐ Finish addressing invitations and announcements
- ☐ Finalize wardrobe for showers, pre-wedding parties, and honey-moon.
- ☐ Shop for gifts for bridal party
- ☐ Shop for accessories, such as shoes, stockings, garter, purse, cake knife, candles, and guest registration book
- ☐ Choose wedding rings, and arrange for engraving
- ☐ Plan you bridesmaid's party
- ☐ Schedule an appointment with your hairdresser and make-up consultant
- ☐ Finalize and verify all details with service providers
- ☐ Order wedding cake

6 Weeks Before

- ☐ Mail invitations
- ☐ Bride's portrait sitting
- ☐ Confirm all male and female attendants have been fitted for formalwear
- ☐ Schedule rehearsal and inform all who needed to be there
- ☐ Make final menu decisions
- ☐ Discuss wedding photo shots with photographer and videographer
- ☐ Send announcement to newspaper
- ☐ Write thank you notes for gifts

2 Weeks Before

- ☐ Pick up wedding gown, and confirm that it fits properly
- ☐ Take care of blood and medical test, and marriage license
- ☐ Finalize musical selections for the ceremony and reception
- ☐ Finalize seating chart for reception
- ☐ Finish addressing announcements to mail on wedding day

1 Week Before

- ☐ Pick up wedding rings
- ☐ Give final guest count for the reception to your caterer
- ☐ Practice applying make-up for the wedding day, if you're doing it on your own
- ☐ Confirm details with all service providers
- ☐ Verify all bridesmaids and groomsmen have picked up their formalwear
- ☐ Confirm that all attendants know when to arrive at the rehearsal, rehearsal dinner and wedding ceremony
- ☐ Confirm honeymoon plans
- ☐ Make a list of names and pronunciations for the Best Man to mention in his introduction, if appropriate
- ☐ Cancel newspaper and mail for while you're away
- ☐ Pay upcoming bills that will be due while you are away
- ☐ Pack for honeymoon and purchase traveler's checks
- ☐ Arrange to move belongings to new home

1-2 Days Before

- ☐ Review any special seating arrangements with ushers
- ☐ Groom to pick up formalwear
- ☐ Make sure to have marriage license
- ☐ Check all final details with caterer, florist, musicians, etc.

The Night Before

Sleep, sleep, sleep-you have the biggest day of your life ahead of you. You want to look and feel your best. Make time with family, especially parents to share memories of times gone by and to say thank you. Take photos of your last hours at home as a single person. Take some quiet time for yourself. Close your eyes and visualize every step of the coming day. This will relax you and help prevent unforeseen incidents

The morning of…

Have a small meal before leaving for the church don't bring too many personal items to the church less to worry about. MOST IMPORTANT!!!! Stay Calm….if you run behind schedule-take a deep breath and remember that ceremony will wait for you!!!! Your family and friends want to see you shine….not be frazzled because you are running late so, relax….looking, feeling and radiating you happiness is what counts.

THE GROOM'S CHECKLIST:

6 to 12 Months Prior

- ☐ Purchase the Bride's Engagement Ring
- ☐ Discuss with Fiancée the Date & Type of Wedding
- ☐ Start on Your Guest List
- ☐ Select your Best Man & Ushers
- ☐ Start planning and making Arrangements for the Honeymoon
- ☐ Discuss and plan with your Fiancée your new home together, if she is moving in with you begin cleaning out closets, cupboards, and drawers to make room for your bride.
- ☐ Make arrangements with local hotels to set aside rooms for out of guests, or guests who might over indulge at the reception.

4 Months Prior

- ☐ Shop for Wedding Rings
- ☐ Complete your Guest List, including Full Names, Addresses, and Phone Numbers
- ☐ Check requirements for Blood Tests and Marriage License
- ☐ Select and Order the Men's Wedding Attire
- ☐ Finalize Honeymoon Plans - do not forget to send in your Deposits!!

2 Months Prior

- ☐ Meet with the Officiant to Finalize Ceremony Details
- ☐ Assist Parents with Plans for the Rehearsal Dinner
- ☐ Discuss the amount and Financial Arrangements for the flowers, which are normally the Groom's responsibility.

1 Month Prior

- ☐ Schedule Final Fittings for Tuxedos, and make sure all Wedding Attire has been ordered
- ☐ Purchase Gifts for Best Man and Ushers
- ☐ Purchase a Gift for your Bride, if Gifts are being exchanged
- ☐ Take care of Business and Legal Affairs, such as adding Bride's name to Insurance Policies, Medical Plans; add Bride's name to Checking Accounts.
- ☐ Reconfirm accommodations for guests

2 Weeks Prior

- ☐ Together with your Bride to Be, file for your Marriage License
- ☐ Arrange Wedding Day Transportation
- ☐ If moving, get a change of address card to the Post Office on in New Home
- ☐ If you are not moving - continue with cleaning and reorganizing your home and help your Fiancée with the moving of her things

1 Week Prior

- ☐ Discuss All Final Details with Fiancée, offer to Assist Where & When Needed
- ☐ Pick up and Try On Wedding Attire
- ☐ Make sure Best Man & Ushers get their Wedding Attire
- ☐ Pack Clothes for your Honeymoon
- ☐ Reconfirm All Honeymoon Reservations - If flying, Make Sure you have the Plane Tickets
- ☐ Have your Hair Cut

- [ ] Make sure your Attendants are at the Rehearsal, and know their Duties
- [ ] Make sure your Ushers are aware of Special Seating Arrangements
- [ ] Make sure your luggage is in the Car or Hotel where you will stay your First Night
- [ ] Bring your Wedding License to the Officiant at Rehearsal, be sure it is **filled out properly** so it can be signed and returned to you after your Wedding
- [ ] Attend your Rehearsal Dinner - Relax and Enjoy Yourself!
- [ ] Go to bed early, you want to look and feel your best!

The Wedding Day

- [ ] Be sure to have a Good Breakfast
- [ ] Time to Get Dressed: Start at least One Hour before the Ceremony
- [ ] Give the Best Man the Bride's Wedding Ring
- [ ] Prepare the Officiant's Fee or Gift in an Envelope, and give it to the Best Man so he can present it after the ceremony.
- [ ] Don't Forget the Marriage License, Make sure it's Signed by Officiant, & Witnesses
- [ ] Dance First with your Bride, then both Mothers, and then Bridesmaids
- [ ] Just Before leaving the Reception, Thank the Bride's Parents
- [ ] Say Goodbye to your Parents

After the Wedding Day

On the first day of the honeymoon send flowers expressing your appreciation and thanking the bride's parents again for a beautiful wedding & reception. Remember to treat your wife with dignity, love, and respect. Don't forget to surprise her with thoughtful gift.

Chapter Two

<u>WHAT TO ASK VENDORS:</u>

It helps to know what questions to ask when you are visiting wedding vendors such as photographers, florist, and venues. It can mean the difference of saving both time and money. All professional and well established vendors should be able to answer each question accurately.

<u>Questions to Ask Reception Sites</u>

- What is the rental fee? What exactly does it include?
- What is the maximum attendance the room or area can handle - for a seated dinner, buffet, or hors d'oeuvre reception?
- Is the reception site to be shared with another wedding group? How are the facilities divided? How is privacy ensured?
- For how many hours does the rental fee reserve the space? Are there charges for overtime? When do they begin?
- Are there any restrictions on when the site is available? Any price discounts for certain time periods, days of the week?
- Do you have a piano, other musical instrument on the premises? Is there any charge for use?
- Are there any regulations concerning the type of music; number of musicians; duration of the music?
- Are there regulations on decorations, flowers, photography?

- Do you have air conditioning (for warm weather weddings)? Adequate heating (for winter and early spring nuptials)?
- Do you have an in-house caterer or preferred list of caterers? Can I bring in the caterer of my choice? What are your liquor requirements?
- Do you have any liability insurance in the event a guest is injured?
- Do you have an enclosed and adequate kitchen facility? (Caterers may add surcharges for appliances - a stove, refrigerator, etc.)
- Can the site be used for the ceremony?
- Is there a dance floor? Is dancing allowed? Where?
- Are there any additional charges for required services (i.e. security guards, parking attendants, doormen, lawn workers, etc.)?
- Can you confirm the reservation in a letter that will outline all the details, including the room assignment?
- What are the deposit and refund requirements?
- Is there adequate parking for my guests? Will they be charged? Can these charges be waived?
- Are there rooms available where we can change into wedding attire, going-away clothes?
- Do you have a microphone?
- Can we review staging, lighting, audio and video needs?
- Is there a comfortable area for guests to await our arrival from the ceremony site? Can hors d'oeuvres and drinks be served there?
- Where is the best place to set up the receiving line?
- What is the name of the banquet manager? Will he or she be on hand that day? If not, who will be in charge?
- Is a security deposit required? How much is it? When can I expect a refund?
- Do you provide tables? What kind - round, oblong, and how many to a table? Chairs?
- Do you have a floor plan available for sketching the reception layout? Where will the cake table, gift table, bride's table be located?

- Are table covers/skirts available? Colors available?
- What are the colors of the facility?

Questions for Videographers

What does the video package include?

- Unedited tape
- Multi-camera
- Montage of stills
- Titles
- Narration
- Background music
- Close-up shots
- Interviews with family, wedding party, guests
- Can interviews be interspersed throughout the tape?
- Can your taping be serious or humorous? Are creative options available?
- Discuss costs. Work out a clear payment schedule.
- Obtain an itemized agreement that lists everything included in the package and the total cost.
- How many tapes come with the package? What is the cost for extra tapes?
- How is the tape packaged professionally? Does it have a case, album, printed labels?
- Is a deposit required? If so, how much?
- How many hours does the price include?
- Can he/she arrive early to capture last-minute preparations, moments with family members and unexpected situations?
- How is overtime handled?
- Does the videographer maintain the tape? If so, how long?
- How far in advance must reservations be made?
- What is the cancellation policy?
- Can you select the background music, and is there a large selection to choose from?

- Is broadcast-quality editing equipment used?
- What kind of camera equipment will be used? Is it consumer or commercial quality equipment?
- What is the format? (Should be hi-8 or super VHS)
- Will there be sufficient light available at the time and location of the ceremony?
- Sound: The best videographers are using a wireless microphone (example: True Diversity) to get clean, clear audio.
- Is the person who is showing you the videos the same person who will be shooting your wedding?
- Make sure you know who is taping the wedding, and get it in writing.
- Is the videographer familiar with the site you have selected?
- What will the videographer's attire be?

Questions for the Photographer

A good time to begin shopping for a photographer and/or videographer is nine to twelve months before the wedding. Begin the search with the recommendations received from your family and friends. Have them look through the individual photographer's wedding albums, checking for styles and formats that they like best.

- Do the photographs have a sharp, crisp quality?
- Does the photographer offer retouching or any special effects?
- Check for a mix of shots – what is the level of the photographer's creativity?
- Is there visible emotion in subject matter, composition, or people?
- Will he/she design the album specifically for them?
- How long does the photographer keep the negatives?
- Can he/she arrive early to capture the last-minute preparations, moments with family, and other "little" events that make the day so special?
- Can they see the proofs online? If so, will the web address be available to family and friends? Can they order online?
- Is there an extra charge for the proofs?

- Discuss costs. What is their payment plan? Obtain an itemized agreement that lists everything included in the package they are purchasing and what the total cost will be.
- Does the quoted price include a finished album? What is the price for additional albums? Will they provide a Parent's album free of charge?
- Is the person who is showing you the photos the same person that will be photographing their wedding?
- If not, can you meet "the actual" photographer?
- Will there be an assistant? If yes, is there an additional charge for this person?
- If applicable, what is the charge for a Bridal Portrait? When should this be done? What is the cost for a Bride and Groom Portrait?
- Do you have confidence that this person will perform in a professional manner and be inconspicuous as well as deliver memorable photographs of their special day?

Questions to Ask Florists

- Are you familiar with the site(s)? If not, will you arrange to visit the site(s) with me?
- May I see photographs of your work, sketches, or sample wedding albums?
- Can you also provide aisle runners, stanchions, candelabra, or any other needs I have that the site cannot provide?
- Are there any restrictions of the kinds of decorations I may use at my ceremony and reception sites (candles-fire laws; colors-liturgical reasons; delivery and setup-conflicts with other services or parties)?
- Are there any limitations on my choices of flowers (bridesmaids' gowns, the decor of the site, lighting or the lack of it, seasonal availability, or budget considerations)?
- Given my locations, time of day, season of the year, and planned reception activities, do I need flowers that are particu-

larly hardy, which will retain their appearance under less than ideal conditions?

- Can you help me enhance a wedding tone or mood with flowers: casual, country, formal, sophistication, dramatic?
- Can you make me a preliminary list of what you think I'll need in numbers of bouquets, arrangements, boutonnieres, and so on?
- When will the flowers be delivered? Is there a delivery fee?
- Who is to receive them? Is there a set-up fee?
- What are your guarantees regarding freshness, availability and substitutions?
- What is the estimated total cost of all my selections?
- What is your payment and cancellation policy?

Questions to ask the potential Disk Jockey

- Do you belong to any professional associations or trade groups?
- How long have you been a Disk Jockey?
- How many venues have you played?
- What is your typical play list like? How many songs?
- Do you take requests?
- Will you supply us with a list of references that they may call upon?
- Do you have professional equipment, or personal?
- Do you supply emergency power / back-up systems?
- Are we guaranteed the Disk Jockey of our choice for our venue?
- What is your usual wedding attire?
- Can we choose the actual songs you will play?
- What styles can you provide?
- How long are your sets / breaks (how often are they?)
- What are your charges determined by? By-the-set price or hourly?
- What is an average time you play for weddings?
- What is your overtime charge?
- What is your set-up time?

- Do you play for ceremonies as well?
- If so, how much do you charge for this service?
- Do you carry liability insurance? If so, will you provide a copy for their records?

Ceremony Sites and Inspection Questions

- Does the church/synagogue have any special rules or traditions that you should know about? Can you write your vows, personalize your ceremony?
- What are the parameters?
- What will be the time limitations on your wedding day? Is there a ceremony preceding or following yours? This should be checked again, two weeks prior to your wedding date.
- Is there a lounge or other setting suitable for photographs? Is there a rest area where other members of your party can relax, should there be some unforeseen delay?
- Who will be your musician? Are you allowed to provide your own musician? Soloist? Music selections?
- What kind of monetary obligations are there? Are you expected to pay for wedding ceremony services, or is a donation more traditional?
- If your ceremony is to be held somewhere other than a church/synagogue (a hotel for instance), what are your obligations to the officiator?
- Is it acceptable to tape record, video or to take flash pictures of the ceremony? Are there facilities for this?
- Aisle runners and length of aisle - what is available and do you wish to use them?
- Where are the flowers to be positioned? What is the best time for them to be delivered? Are there candelabras, candles, unity stand available?
- Are there to be any special seating arrangements for close family members and friends? How is this to be handled?

Questions to Ask Bridal Shops

- When can I expect to have the first fitting?
- How long will the alterations take and how much will they cost?
- How far in advance of the wedding day will the gown be delivered?
- What happens if the gown I choose is out of stock or not available?
- What is your refund policy?
- What is the payment schedule? (How much is the deposit, and when is it due? When is the balance due?) What is the method of payment (i.e. cash, personal check, certified check, credit-card)?

Questions to ask of the Baker

- Do you have photographs we can see of cakes that you have made in the past?
- Can you create the cake they want, even though it may be unique or unusual?
- Can you create flowers or other decorations from sugar molds or frostings?
- Can the tiers be made of different combinations of cake and filling?
- What flavors of cake, filling and frostings are available?
- Do you provide samples to taste?
- Do you make Groom's cakes?
- If we use fresh flowers, who will purchase/add them? You? Our florist? If you do, what is the additional charge?
- $$$May we see a schedule of prices?
- Do you charge a flat per cake fee, or is it by the slice/guest?
- What are the different charges for various frostings, such as fondant, butter cream, etc?
- Do you sell cake toppers?
- Do you sell personalized cake boxes, if we decide to use them?

- Do you sell sheet cakes to supplement the decorated cake to provide their guests with extra servings?
- What is the cost of each of these cakes?
- Do you charge a delivery and/or set-up fee? How much is it?
- If you are delivering the cake, what is the delivery person's attire?
- What is your deposit and when is it due?
- What are your payment terms?
- When will you have the contract ready to sign?
- When must supports (pillars, columns, liqueur glasses) and decorations (plates, fountains, etc.) be returned?
- Do you require returned items to be washed first?
- When is the absolute last date by which they need to give you the final guest count?
- What will you do should an accident occur and the cake is destroyed or dropped?
- What are your back-up plans?
- Will you drape the cake table?
- What type of linens do you use?
- Will you provide a box should there be leftover cake?
- May we see your Health Department certificate (every baker is required by law to have one)

Venue Inspection Questions:

1. **Availability**--When is the room available? By when must it be cleared?
2. **Condition of room.**
3. **Aesthetics**--What are the colors and patterns in the carpet? Walls? Ceiling?
4. **Chandeliers**--Will they cause projection/rigging problems? Placement and clearance from floor?
5. **Tables and chairs**--What quantity of which sizes? What do banquet chairs look like?
6. **Linens**--What sizes and colors of tablecloths and napkins?
7. **Dimensions and floor plans**
8. **How will room(s) be set up?**

9. **Catering**--Who? Location of the kitchen and service doors..
10. **Lighting**--Type of light fixtures and locations of controls. Is there a remote controller? Is there track lighting? Locations?
11. **Sound**--What type of in-house system? Quality? What are the acoustics of the room? Will room require sound? Flown or ground support? Will delay stacks be needed? Front or side fill? Monitors?
12. **Temperature**--Control?
13. **Loading dock**--Height? Restrictions? How many trucks can be accommodated? Can space be reserved?

Venue Inspection Questions:

1. **Availability**--When is room available? By when must it be cleared?
2. **Condition of room.**
3. **Aesthetics**--What are the colors and patterns in the carpet? Walls? Ceiling?
4. **Chandeliers**--Will they cause projection/rigging problems? Placement and clearance from floor?
5. **Tables and chairs**--What quantity of which sizes? What do banquet chairs look like?
6. **Linens**--What sizes and colors of tablecloths and napkins?
7. **Dimensions and floor plans**
8. **How will room(s) be set up?**
9. **Catering**--Who? Location of the kitchen and service doors..
10. **Lighting**--Type of light fixtures and locations of controls. Is there a remote controller? Is there track lighting? Locations?
11. **Sound**--What type of in-house system? Quality? What are the acoustics of the room? Will room require sound? Flown or ground support? Will delay stacks be needed? Front or side fill? Monitors?
12. **Temperature**--Control?
13. **Loading dock**--Height? Restrictions? How many trucks can be accommodated? Can space be reserved?

14. **Access from dock to room**--Distance? Corners in halls? Dimensions of the smallest door. Ceiling clearance form dock to room?
15. **Truck parking**--Is there vehicle marshaling space? If not, where is parking? Cost?
16. **Audiovisual**--Who is in house? Capabilities? Competitively priced?
17. **Rigging points**--Where are they? Rigging restrictions?
18. **Projection capability**--Is there a booth? Are there permanent screens? What is a good placement for screens? Will I-mag be needed?
19. **Electrical**--Is there a disconnect? More than one? Where? Capacity: single-phase or three-phase?
20. **Staging**--Sizes, type and heights? How good is it? What color skirting? Steps: with and without railings? What would be a good placement for the stage?
21. **Air walls**--Locations? Sound buffer?
22. **ADA-compliant?**
23. **23.**.Charges--Are there hidden charges? Electrical? Rigging? Dock?
24. **Hospitality**--Are water/coffee stations available? Deli buffet for crew? Who pays for it and how?
25. **Rest rooms**--Locations and capacity?
26. **Foyer**--Capacity, look, floor plan?
27. **Security**--Procedures? Is there a theft problem with the property? Access to security for equipment? Cost? Will security be needed during event? From whom?
28. **Safety**-- What are fire code requirements specific to this room? Who are the first responders on property? Policy regarding vehicles in the building? Policy regarding fog or smoke machines? (Smoke detectors?) Policy regarding live animals?

Chapter Three

DUTIES & RESPONSIBILITIES OF THE WEDDING PARTY:

This chapter discusses the roles of the wedding party and their responsibilities. Listed is a detailed list of duties for each member of the wedding party. This list should be given to each member perhaps when the person is first selected as a member. It establishes responsibilities so that there is no gray area as to the role of the member.

Best Man

- Spread the word about where the couple is registered
- Give groom bachelor party (plan, invite guests)
- Pay for rental of own tux
- Ensure groom arrives on time at the ceremony
- Keep bride's ring until minister asks for it on day of wedding
- Help groom get dressed before wedding
- Help groom remain calm prior to ceremony
- Stand beside groom during ceremony
- Make first toast at the reception
- Offer to return the groom's wedding attire to the formalwear store

Bridesmaids

- Help choose the bridesmaid dresses if possible (geographically)
- Spread the word about where the couple is registered
- Buy own bridesmaid dress and accessories
- Stand beside maid of honor during ceremony

Flower Girl

- Precedes the bride, tossing paper flowers or fresh flower petals down the aisle (ask if your ceremony site allows fresh flowers to be dropped)
- Stand beside the bridesmaids during ceremony

Greeters/Host and Hostess (Reception)

- Pick up the guest book and pen at the end of the ceremony and put at entrance of reception hall
- Make sure reception area setup looks OK (cake? band/DJ there? centerpieces set out?)
- Greet guests as they enter reception and tell them where party, gift table, and guest book are

Groomsman

- Spread the word about where the couple is registered
- Pay for rental of own tux
- Stand beside best man during ceremony

Guest Book Attendant

- Stand by guest book for people to sign prior to ceremony
- Give out favors and birdseed roses at reception

Maid/Matron of Honor
(A Matron of Honor is married; a Maid of Honor is not.)

- Help bride choose a wedding dress
- Help choose the bridesmaid dresses
- Buy own bridesmaid dress and accessories
- Assist bride with wedding plans if asked
- Help the bride address invitations, if she needs it
- Spread the word about where the couple is registered
- Give bride a bridal shower and be present at any other showers that may be thrown for her
- Help bride get dressed before wedding
- Help bride remain calm prior to ceremony
- Keeps groom's ring until minister asks for it on day of wedding
- Stand beside bride during ceremony
- Rearrange the bride's wedding gown train during the ceremony as necessary
- Hold the bouquet and possibly gloves during the exchanging of the rings until after the kiss
- Help the bride get out of her gown and into traveling clothes, if the bride and groom are leaving for their honeymoon right after the reception
- Help the bride's mother get all the wedding gifts to the couple's new home while the couple is on their honeymoon

Mistress of Ceremonies

- Make sure attendants know what they're doing, where and when at the rehearsal
- Ceremony duties:
    - ☐ Help florist give out corsages; ensure everyone gets a flower that should
    - ☐ Ensure centerpiece flowers, unity candles, pew bows, etc. are in place
    - ☐ Get lighter from minister for unity candles
    - ☐ Put guest book and pen at church entrance
    - ☐ Make sure videographer/photographer are set up okay
    - ☐ Give programs to the ushers

- ☐ Tell family members to hang around for quick pictures immediately after the ceremony
- Reception duties:
  - ☐ Try to ensure that no one leaves with disposable cameras
  - ☐ Bring basket of birdseed/bubbles/etc. and give to person who will hand them out
  - ☐ Help mother of bride stay sane and get everything to take home afterwards

MC (Reception) -- family member, friend, DJ, or band leader

- Announce wedding party when they arrive at reception
- Do announcing of the dances, garter and bouquet toss, and final dance

Parents of Bride

- Put couple's luggage in limo
- Bring home items from ceremony (flowers, leftover programs, unity candles, etc.)
- Bring home items from reception (toasting glasses, cake knife and server, gifts, disposable cameras, leftover birdseed roses and favors, centerpieces, cake topper, top layer of cake, etc.)
- Ensure caterer puts food basket in limo at end of reception couple to eat at the hotel

Personal Attendant

- Help bride get dressed
- Carry bride's emergency kit to the reception
- Give out favors and birdseed/bubbles/etc. at reception
- Give emergency kit to bride's mom at the end of reception

Readers

- Read scripture, poetry, or prose selections during the wedding ceremony

Ring Bearer

- Walk down the aisle carrying the rings (or fake ones) secured to a satin pillow
- Stand beside groomsmen during ceremony

Ushers

- Pay for rental of own tux (or they could just wear suits)
- Greet all guests at the ceremony, then ask which family they represent and seat accordingly (optional - traditionally bride's family/friends on left and groom's family/friends on the right of the center aisle; however, if it is expected that this seating arrangement will be very uneven, the ushers can seat guests wherever)
- Unroll the aisle runner after the bride's mother is seated
- Usher mothers and grandmothers out after ceremony and dismiss guests aisle by aisle (optional - guests can be left to dismiss themselves too)

Chapter Four

WEDDING ATTIRE EDIQUETTE:

It is important to know proper attire etiquette (formal, informal, casual, etc.) and when it is applied. Dress your wedding party appropriately for the occasion by using the following guidelines.

Him

- Casual (Informal) Daytime Attire: Dress shirt and pants, preferably a sports jacket.
- Casual (Informal) Evening Attire: Suit
- Cocktail (Semi-Formal) Daytime Attire: Suit
- Cocktail (Semi-Formal) Evening Attire: Dark suit
- Black Tie (Formal) Daytime Attire: Dark suit and tie
- Black Tie (Formal) Evening Attire: Tuxedo or dark suits if women wear short dresses.
- White Tie (Ultra-formal) Evening Attire: White tie, cummerbund, vest and shirt.

Her

- Casual (Informal) Daytime Attire: Short dress or suit (business attire is acceptable)
- Casual (Informal) Evening Attire: Cocktail dress
- Cocktail (Semi-Formal) Daytime Attire: Short dress or suit

- Cocktail (Semi-Formal) Evening Attire: Cocktail dress
- Black Tie (Formal) Daytime Attire: Short dress or suit. Hats and gloves optional
- Black Tie (Formal) Evening Attire: Long or dressy short cocktail (beading, glam accessories, wrap)
- White Tie (Ultra-formal) Evening Attire: Long gown, extra glitz

A quick recap of Do's and Don'ts for Him and Her:

Him

- Do wear a dark suit, with a tie if the wedding is after 6 PM, and doesn't say "Black Tie."
- Do use good judgment if the invitation doesn't specify the formality of the event. A dark suit and conservative tie will take you just about anywhere.
- Don't try to get cute with a tuxedo. A black tuxedo with white shirt and black bow tie is the best way to go. In addition, trendier parties, location people might be more accepting of breaking with tradition.
- Don't wear a tuxedo during the day time, regardless of the formality of the event.

Her

- Do wear something feminine and appropriate, out of respect for your hosts. Club wear, overtly sexy clothing (strapless, see-through, etc) doesn't belong at a wedding. If you have to ask if it is appropriate, it probably is not.
- Do take off gloves to eat or drink.
- Don't wear black or sequins during the daytime.
- Don't worry about wearing the same colors as the bridesmaids or mothers. You cannot possibly coordinate with everyone in the wedding party.

- Don't wear opera-length gloves (to top of arm) with anything but sleeveless or strapless gowns.
- Do use good judgment if the invitation doesn't specify the formality of the event. A pastel suit or soft floral dress for daytime or a little black dress for evening (after 6 p.m.) will take you almost anywhere.

Chapter Five

FLOWERS:

This chapter lists the different uses of flowers and the types of wedding flowers. The next chapter will list their seasons in a useful chart. One of the biggest areas of planning a wedding is flowers. Flowers can quickly add up to be rather expensive especially if the flower of choice is out of season. This information will allow you to better select you wedding flowers based on your needs and budget.

Flower Uses:

Personal Flowers...

- Bridal Bouquet
- Bridal Tossing Bouquet
- Maid of Honor Bouquet
- Bridesmaids' Bouquets
- Corsages for Mothers & Grandmothers
- Flower Girls and/or Junior Bridesmaids' Bouquets
- Boutonnieres for Groom, Groomsmen, Ushers, Fathers, Grandfathers & Ring bearer

Ceremony Flowers...

- Altar Flowers

- Aisle Arrangements

- Pew Ends

Reception Site Flowers...

- Guest Book Table

- Individual Table Centerpieces for Guests

- Head Table Centerpieces

- Buffet Tables

- Bar Centerpiece

- Cocktail Tables

- Serving Trays for Cocktails and Drinks

- Cake Table

If the wedding is held in the bride or groom's house...

- Bathrooms

- Arrangements throughout the house

If you have an unlimited budget, here are some more flowers designs you might want to consider having...

- Guest Reception Line

- Flowers for the Brides Hair

- Flowers for the Bridesmaids'' and Flower Girls Hair

- Cake Knife Corsage

- Gift Table Arrangement

- Floral Chair Garlands for the Bride and Groom

- Door Wreaths
- Pillar Arrangements
- Floral napkin holder

Types of Wedding Flowers

Roses *

- **Bridal Pink:** bright pink
- **Candia**: creamy white with dark pink edges
- **Champaign**: antique ivory
- **Darling:** creamy peach
- **Delores**: soft pink
- **Jacaranda**: hot pink
- **Lady Diana**: pale peach
- **Jacqueline Kennedy**: small, true-red
- **Madame Delhard**: rich, velvety red (French)
- **Sterling Silver:** small, lavender
- **Sonia:** bright peach

Orchids *

- **Catlaya**: usually, white with shades of pink or lavender in each petal's center – larger than other orchids
- **Cymbidium**: smaller than Japhet orchids, with curly edge only at the center
- **Dendrobium**: miniature orchids that come in a spray*
- **Japhet**: large, with curly edge all over. They often have a yellow throat

- **Phalaenopsis**: round-edged, white, with reddish throat

spray: long spikes, covered with tiny orchid-like flowers. These are very expensive and are available in winter.

Lillies *

- **Alstroemeria:** miniature lily in a variety of colors
- **Calla**: very large, long white flowers on thick stalks
- **Day Lillies:** usually in shades of cream, orange, red or yellow, with a variety of stem lengths
- **Lily of the Valley**: small, white blooms that look like tiny bells
- **Rubrium**: star flowers, in a variety of colors
- **Zephyr Lily**: smaller than most lilies, available in white, yellow and Shadeofpink

Miscellaneous Flowers *

- **Amaryllis**: deep red and/or white. Similar in shape to the long stemmed lily
- **Anemones**: similar to a poppy, available in white, blue, red-violet and yellow
- **Anthuriums**: a true-red flower with a heart-shaped bloom and large stamen
- **Asters**: white, pin, rose or purple
- **Baby's Breath**: fine, delicate, tiny flowers that is usually white
- **Bachelor Buttons**: like tiny carnations, available in white, pink, red or blue
- **Canterbury Bells:** like little bells, usually blue, purple or pink
- **Carnations**: usually an inexpensive, common flower that comes in a variety of colors – available year round

- **Chrysanthemums:** white, yellow and red. Many different shapes and sizes

- **Daffodils:** pretty and common flower available in many colors

- **Daisy:** popular flower, similar to, but smaller than, a chrysanthemum – available in white or yellow, with a yellow center

- **Delphinium:** long spikes of flowers with lacy foliage – available in white, rose, lavender or blue

- **Forget-me-not:** pretty, dainty blue flower with a yellow or white center

- **Freesia:** delicate flower in white, yellow, pink, orange, lavender or red

- **Gardenia:** white flower with dark green leaves – very fragrant

- **Gerbera Daisies:** giant version of the common daisy – available in a variety of colors

- **Gladiolus:** long stalks, covered in bright blooms, ranging from a variety of colors, including white, red, purple and yellow

- **Iris:** long stalks, large petals, two drop down. Available in white, blue, violet, yellow and orange

- **Lilac:** stalks with many tiny white or lavender flowers

- **Ranuculus:** a rose look-alike, but much less expensive. Available in red, pink and yellow

- **Stattice:** bunches of tiny white or purple blossoms

- **Stephanotis:** small, white trumpet-shaped flowers which grow on vines

- **Straw Flowers:** straw-like petals, shaped like daisies. Available in white, yellow, orange or red

- **Violets:** tiny flowers available in white, blue and purple

Chapter Six

FLOWER SEASONS:

The "x" marks the flower's in-season. The cost of some flowers may be significantly higher during their off-season.

Flowers	Winter	Spring	Summer	Fall
Allium		X	X	
Alstroemeria	X	X	X	X
Amaryllis	X		X	
Anemone	X	X		X
Aster	X	X	X	X
Baby's Breath	X	X	X	X
Bachelor's Button	X	X	X	X
Billy Buttons		X	X	
Bird of Paradise	X	X	X	X
Bouvardia	X	X	X	X
Calla Lily	X	X	X	X
Carnation	X	X	X	X
Celosia		X	X	

Flowers	Winter	Spring	Summer	Fall
Chrysanthemum	X	X	X	X
Daffodils		X		
Dahlia			X	X
Delphinium			X	X
Eucalyptus	X	X	X	X
Freesia	X	X	X	X
Gardenia	X	X	X	X
Gladiolus	X	X	X	X
Iris	X	X	X	X
Liatris		X	X	X
Lily	X	X	X	X
Lily of Valley		X		
Lisianthus		X	X	X
Narcissus	X	X		X
Nerine	X	X	X	X
Orchid (cattleya)	X	X	X	X
Orchid (Cymbidium)	X	X	X	X
Peony		X		
Pincushion			X	
Protea		X		X
Queen Anne's Lace			X	
Ranunculus		X		
Rose	X	X	X	X
Saponaria			X	

Flowers	Winter	Spring	Summer	Fall
Snapdragon		X	X	X
Speedwell			X	
Star of Bethleham	X			X
Statice	X	X	X	X
Stephanotis	X	X	X	X
Stock	X	X	X	X
Sunflower		X	X	
Sweet Pea		X		
Tuberose			X	X
Tulip	X	X		
Waxflower	X	X		

Chapter Seven

WEDDING COST ESTIMATION:

One of the most important areas in wedding planning is the cost. Planning cannot be set into motion without a solid idea of what are the costs. It is very important to be realistic with the wedding costs and to give great thought to it. This chapter lists the typical cost of each area of wedding planning followed by a worksheet to analyze the wedding budget in the Chapter eight.

Wedding Flower Fees:

- **Bride's Bouquet:**
  Price Range: $60 - $500

- **Tossing Bouquet:**
  If the bride plans on preserving her bridal bouquet, she should consider having a florist make a smaller, less expensive bouquet specifically for tossing.
  Price Range: $10 - $30

- **Maid of Honor's Bouquet:**
  Price Range: $25 - $75

- **Bridesmaids Bouquet:**
  Price Range: $15 - $60

- **Maid of Honor / Bridesmaids' Hairpiece:**
  Price Range: $8 - $25

- **Flower Girl's Hairpiece:**
  Price Range: $8 - $25

- **Family Members' Corsages:**
  Price Range: $10 - $25

- **Groom's Boutonniere:**
  Price Range: $4 - $10

- **Ushers and Other Family Members' Boutonnieres:**
  Price Range: $3 - $7

- **Flowers for the Main Altar:**
  The purpose of flowers at the main altar is to direct the guests' visual attention toward the front of the church or synagogue and to the bridal couple.
  Price Range: $50 - $1,000

- **Altar Candelabra:**
  In a candlelight ceremony, the candelabra may be decorated with flowers or greens for a dramatic effect.
  Price Range: $25 - $50

- **Aisle Pews:**
  Flowers, candles or ribbons are often used to mark the aisle pews and add color.
  Price Range: $5 - $40

- **Reception Site:**
  Price Range: $300 - $1,500

- **Head Table:**
  The head table is where the wedding party will sit during the reception. This important table should be decorated with a larger or more dramatic centerpiece than the guest tables.
  Price Range: $50 - $300

- **Guest Tables:**
  At a reception where guests are seated, a small flower arrangement may be placed on each table.
  Price Range: $10 - $60

- **Buffet Table:**
  If buffet tables are used, have some type of floral arrangement on the tables to add color and beauty to your display of food.
  Price Range: $50 - $300

- **Punch Table:**
  If a punch table is used, put an assortment of greens or a small arrangement of flowers.
  Price Range: $10 - $50

- **Cake Table:**
  Price Range: $15 - $25

- **Cake Knife:**
  Decorate the cake knife with a white satin ribbon and/or flowers.
  Price Range: $5 - $20

- **Toasting Glasses:**
  Tie small flowers with white ribbons on the stems of your champagne glasses.
  Price Range: $10 - $30

- **Floral Delivery & Set-up Fee:**
  Price Range: $25 - $100

- **Table Centerpieces:**
  Each of the tables at the reception, including the head table, should be decorated with a centerpiece.
  Price Range: $5 - $30

- **Balloons:**
  Balloons are often used to decorate a reception site.
  Price Range: $75 - $500

Ceremony Site Fee

The ceremony site fee is the fee to rent the facility for the couple's wedding.

Tips to save money: Have the ceremony at the same facility as the reception to save on the second venue rental fee. Set a realistic guest list and stick to it. At a church or temple, ask if there is another wedding that day and share the cost of the floral arrangements for the site with the other Bride. If you belong to a church or temple, the rental fees could be less. At a garden wedding, have the guests stand rather than renting chairs.

Price Range: $100 - $800

Officiant's fee

The officiant's fee is the fee paid to whoever performs the wedding ceremony.

Things to consider: Some officiants may not accept payment directly. If a fee is refused, send a donation to the officiant's church, synagogue or favorite charity.

Price Range: $50 - $500

Officiant's Gratuity

The officiant's gratuity is a discretionary amount of money given to the officiant.

Things to consider: This amount should depend on the couple's relationship with the officiant and the amount of time he/she has spent with them prior to the wedding ceremony.

Price Range: $25 - $250

Guest Book, Pen, Penholder

The guest book is the formal register of all who attended the wedding ceremony and/or reception.

Things to consider: Make sure there are multiple pens available in case one runs out of ink, or is pocketed by mistake.

Price Range: $10 - $75

Ring Bearer's Pillow

The Ring Bearer, usually a young boy between the ages of 4 and 8, carries the Bride and Groom's rings, or mock rings, on a pillow down the aisle during the wedding procession to the altar.

Things to consider: If the Ring Bearer is very young (less than 7 years old), place mock rings on the pillow to prevent the loss of the real rings. Have the Best Man and the Maid of Honor hold/carry the real rings to the altar. If mock rings are used on the Ring Bearer's pillow, instruct the Ring Bearer's guardian to put the pillow out of sight during the recessional so that the guests do not see the fake rings.

Price Range: $5 - $35

Flower Girl's Basket

The Flower Girl, usually a young girl between the ages of 4 and 8, carries a basket filled with either flowers, flower petals (most often rose petals), or paper petals which she tosses as she walks down the aisle towards the altar.

Tips to save money: Ask the florist the Bride has chosen if you can borrow a basket. Decorate with silk flowers and white ribbons. Attach a large white bow.

Price Range: $5 - $35

Bride's Wedding Gown

Tips to save money: Consider renting a gown or buying a second-hand one. A rented gown costs around 40% to 60% of the new, retail price. Borrowing a family member's gown is another alternative. There are many discount stores such as David's Bridal which sell discounted, new, gowns.

Price Range: $300 - $3,000

Alterations

Alterations may be necessary in order to have the gown fit perfectly.

Tips to save money: Consider hiring an independent tailor rather than using the alterations department of the bridal shop. Their fees are usually lower than those of the boutiques.

Price Range: $50 - $150

Headpiece & Veil

This can be a tiara, a ring of flowers, a headband covered in satin and/or tulle or anything the veil attaches to.

Tips to save money: Some boutiques offer a free headpiece and veil with the purchase of a wedding gown and bridesmaid's dresses. Make sure you ask before buying the gown.

Price Range: $60 - $250

Gloves

These add an elegant touch, especially with sleeveless, three-quarter length or short-sleeve gowns.

Price Range: $5 - $30

Jewelry

Is an option, if worn at all.

Things to consider: Less is more – perhaps a string of pearls and stud earrings, with a delicate gold chain bracelet.

Price Range: $60 - $1,000

Garter

It is customary for the Bride to wear a garter, just above, or below the knee on her wedding day. After the bouquet is tossed, the Groom removes the garter and tosses it into a crowd of all the single men attending the wedding. Like the bouquet, whoever catches the garter will be the next newlywed.

Price Range: $5 - $15

Shoes

Things to consider: Be sure to have the Bride wear comfortable shoes that she has purchased, and worn, before the wedding. There is nothing worse than sore feet and a limping bride on the dance floor. Make sure the shoes compliment, or match, the wedding gown.

Price Range: $25 - $100

Hairdresser

Things to consider: Have the chosen beautician experiment with styles incorporating the headpiece and veil long before the actual wedding day. On the morning of, the Bride, her Bridesmaids and Flower Girl, along with both the Mothers, can have the stylist do their hair so they have a similar look.

Tips to save money: Negotiate with the hairdresser to have the Bride's style done at no charge, or at a discount, in exchange for bringing the wedding party and Mothers to the salon.

Price Range: $20 - $75 per person

Makeup Artist

Things to consider: Have the Bride, Bridesmaids, and both Mothers done by the same artist, for a consistent look.

Tips to save money: Negotiate for the Bride's makeup to be done at no charge, or for a discount, if the wedding party and Mothers use the same artist.

Price Range: $15 - $25 per person

Manicure and/or Pedicure

Things to consider: For a consistent look, use the same salon and/or the manicurist/pedicurist.

Tips to save money: Negotiate the Bride's manicure/pedicure at no charge, or for a discount, if all Bridesmaids and both Mothers use the same artist or attend the same salon.

Price Range: $10 - $30 per person

Groom's Formal Wear

The Groom should select his formal wear based on the style of the wedding. For semi-formal, or a more traditionally formal wedding, he will need a tuxedo. The most popular colors are black, white or gray.

Tips to save money: Try to negotiate the Groom's tuxedo at no charge, or for a discount, in exchange for having the Groomsmen, both Fathers and the Ring Bearer's tuxedos rented from the same shop.

Price Range: $60 - $120

Bride and Groom's Album

The photo album is the best way for the Bride and Groom to remember and preserve their wedding day.

Things to consider: Hire a photographer who specializes in weddings. Preview several photographers for their individual style and quality before choosing one. Explore the options for album covers, types of packages offered as well as prices and items included, or offered for an additional fee. Take notes when interviewing each photographer so that they can be compared later, in private.

Tips to save money: Select a photographer who charges a flat fee for the entire wedding "shoot" and will allow the Bride and Groom to purchase the negatives. The couple could choose to buy their own album and place the photographs as they prefer, rather than paying the photographer for this service. Ask if there are promotional specials, or specific "deals" being offered.

Price Range: $400 - $3,000

Parent's Album

This is a smaller version of the Bride and Groom's album. Typically, it contains approximately twenty photographs. The couple usually presents one to each set of parents as a gift.

Tips to save money: Try to negotiate with the photographer for, at least, one parent's album at no additional charge, with the purchase of the Bride and Groom's album.

Price Range: $60 - $100

Extra Prints

Additional photographs ordered with the Bride and Groom's album. These are typically given as gifts to family and friends.

Tips to save money: Ask the photographer to sell the negatives. This way, the couple can have prints made at their leisure and for less expense.

Price Range: $3 - $15 / $10 - $25 / $25 - $75

(5" x 7") (8" x 10") (11" x 14")

Videographer

There should be an option of one to three cameras used for the video. Multiple cameras mean more coverage with different angles, rooms and action. Of course, less cameras equals less expensive.

Things to consider: Choose a videographer who specializes in weddings. Interview several and have them demonstrate their product so the Bride and Groom can take notes on quality, clarity, subject matter, sound quality and any additional extras such as fade-out, narration and/or music.

Tips to save money: Interview companies that offer both photography and videography services.

Price Range: $350 - $2,000 / $35 - $60 per overtime hour

Extra Copies: $5 - $35

Invitations

Invitations should be ordered at least 4 months in advance, 5 months if they are to be engraved. They are traditionally issued by the Bride's parents/ however, if the Groom's parents are assuming some of the wedding expenses, consider having them listed on the invitations also. Mail the Invitations 6 – 8 weeks prior to the wedding ceremony.

Things to consider: Order approximately 20% more than the couple's guest count. Allow a *__minimum of 2 weeks__* to address and mail the Invitations, longer if the couple will be using a calligrapher, or if the guest list is over 150.

Tips to save money: Choose paper stock that is reasonable, yet still achieves the overall "look" the couple wishes. Select Invitations that require a single stamp. Order at least 25 extra invitations; mistakes in addressing them can occur, as well as additional people included at the last moment. It will save the cost of reordering a small amount at a premium rate.

Price Range: $0.75 - $5 per Invitation

Related Invitation Fees:

- Response Cards: $0.40 - $0.80 each
- Reception Cards: $0.35 - $0.60 each
- Ceremony Cards: $0.35 - $0.60 each
- Pew Cards: $0.35 - $0.60 each
- Seating / Place Cards: $0.20 - $0.60 each
- Maps: $0.50 - $0.75 each
- Thank – you Notes: $0.35 - $0.50 each
- Stamps: $0.37 - $1.00 each
- Calligraphy: $0.30 - $3.00 each

Reception Site

This venue is where all the Bride and Groom's guests come together to celebrate their new life together as a married couple. The selection of the reception site will depend on: Its availability, price, ambience, proximity to the ceremony site and number of people it will accommodate.

Things to consider: Some hotels will "bump" a couple's event to a less expensive room should a more profitable event occur on the same day. Also, beware of another event in the chosen room that is too close in time. Check with the hotel manager as to their policies, and have the contract you sign state specifically what the venue's promise is and what their remedy will be should anything unforeseen happen.

Tips to save money: Reception sites may waive the corkage and cake cutting fees if they charge a room rental fee. This negotiated point also needs to be specified in the contract and signed by all parties.

Price Range: $300 - $1,000

Related Reception Fees:

- Hors d'oeuvres: $1 - $10 per person
- Main Meal / Caterer: $10 - $60 per person
- Liquor / Beverage: $8 - $25 per person
- -Bartending / Bar set-up: $50 - $375
- Coffee pouring fee: $0.25 - $0.75 per person
- Gratuity: 15% - 18% of total bill
- Party Favors: $1 - $8 per person
- Rose Petals / Rice or
- Birdseed: $0.35 - $1 per person
- Service Provider's Meals: Negotiable point – never pay what is spent on the invited guests $7 - $25 per person
- Parking Fee / Valet: $1.50 - $9 per vehicle

Ceremony Music

There are several "sections" to any wedding ceremony.

- The _Prelude_ is the music played 15 – 30 minutes before the ceremony begins while guests are being seated and is usually either a harpist, organist, or small ensemble.

- The _Processional_ music is played as the wedding party enters the ceremony site and walks down the aisle to the altar.

- The *Ceremony* music is played during the actual ceremony, as the couple indicates.

- The *Recessional* music is played as the wedding party exits the ceremony altar area and returns back down the aisle.

- The *Postlude* music is played while the guests leave the ceremony site.

Tips to save money: If a band is hired for the reception, consider having a few members play at the ceremony itself, such as a flute, guitar and/or vocalist. Consider negotiations for a "package" price. If, on the other hand, a Disk Jockey is hired for the reception, consider having him/her play pre-recorded music selected by the couple for their ceremony.

Price Range: $50 - $400

Reception Music

This will create the ambience at the reception party. Special songs, personally selected by the Bride and Groom, will make their reception unique and memorable. Site restrictions will have to be taken into consideration, as well as the number and ages of their guests and their budget.

Things to consider: Bands are typically more expensive than Disk Jockeys. The couple could save around $200 - $1,000 when hiring a DJ. Ask friends and family if they have heard a band, or been at an event with a particularly memorable Disk Jockey. Always discuss the selection of music to be played before hiring and settle on the "play list," then include it in the contract before it is signed.

Tips to save money: Hire the musicians or Disk Jockey directly, rather than using an entertainment company.

Price Range: $300 - $3,000

Wedding Cake

The wedding cake is usually ordered through a bakery or caterer, although sometimes the reception site includes them in their rental fee. An example would be a hotel or a restaurant.

Things to consider: Variations from baker to baker include: quality, taste, style, creativity, decoration, flavors of cakes, fillings and frosting. Spoilage is a consideration – remember sugared icings last longer than cream frostings.

Tips to save money: Set-up and delivery fees are sometimes negotiable. Check for individuals who bake from their home. Their cost might be less; however quality and reliability are important issues. Some caterers have discounts available for certain bakers. Check with them before ordering from a private venue. Deposits and extra charges for specialty items such as pillars, decorations, plates and/or flowers need to be considered. Always ask if there is a time-limit on returning items to the bakery. Do they use disposable columns and/or plates? This could save on the rental fee as well as eliminate returning items to them.

Price Range: $1 - $8 per person

Related Wedding Cake Fees:

- Delivery and Set-up: $20 - $50
- Cake-cutting: $0.75 - $1.75 per person
- Cake Top: $25 - $150
- Cake Knife: $15 - $120
- Toasting Glasses: $30 - $80

Transportation

It is customary for the bride and her father to ride to the ceremony site together on the wedding day. The bride may choose to include some or all members of the wedding party. Normally a procession to the church begins with the bride's mother and several of the bride's attendants in the first vehicle. If desired, a second vehicle for the rest of the attendants. The bride and her father will go in the last vehicle. This vehicle will also be used to transport the bride and groom to the reception site after the ceremony.

Things to Consider: Make sure the company is fully licensed and has liability insurance. Do not pay the full amount until after the event.

Tips to Save Money: Consider hiring only one large limousine instead of two smaller ones.

Price Range: $35 - $100/hour

Rental Items (The following lists are possible rental items)

Bridal Slip Rental:

The bridal slip is an undergarment which gives the bridal gown its proper shape.

Price Range: $15 - $45

Ceremony Accessories:

Ceremony rental accessories are additional items needed for the ceremony, but not included in the ceremony site fee. They include Aisle Runner (a thin rug made of plastic, paper or cloth extending the length of the aisle), kneeling cushion, arch (Christian wedding: a white lattice or brass arch where the bride and groom exchange their vows, often decorated with flowers and greenery), Chuppah (Jewish wedding: a canopy under which a Jewish ceremony is performed, symbolizing cohabitation and consummation). The couple may also need to consider renting audio equipment, aisle stanchions, candelabra, candle lighters, chairs, heaters, a gift table, and a guest book stand.

Price Range: $100 - $400

Tent / Canopy:

A large tent or canopy may be required for receptions held outdoors to protect wedding party and guests from the sun or rain.

Price Range: $300 - $3,000

Tables / Chairs:

Price Range: $3 - $8/person

Linen / Tableware:

Price Range: $3 - $20/person

Chapter Eight

THE BUDGET:

The average couple will spend \$28,800 on their wedding and has an average engagement of ten months to one year. It is important to have a realistic understanding of what your actual cost will be. Once you know this, then you are more likely to stay within your budget. Listed below is a typical distribution of how your budget should be allocated.

Total Budget

Start by thinking about the total amount of money you and your groom are able to spend. Consider *all* sources: you and your groom, both sets of parents, as well as any other generous family or friends.

Enter total budget: _____

Reception: 50%

This includes:

- ☐ Site fee, if applicable
- ☐ Catering costs (including taxes and tips)
- ☐ Bar (liquor, wine & champagne) and non-alcoholic beverages
- ☐ Wedding Cake
- ☐ Valet parking, if applicable

☐ All transportation for guests, family and bridal party to and from the ceremony site to the reception venue

Enter Reception Budget: _____

(Multiply total budget by 0.5)

Music: 10%

This includes:

☐ Ceremony - harpist, organ music, choir, soloist, etc.
☐ Cocktail hour - Disk Jockey or Band
☐ Reception - Dance music / background music – Disc Jockey or Band

Enter Music Budget: _____

(Multiply total budget by 0.1)

Flowers: 10%

This can become a much greater percentage of the total budget and includes:

☐ Ceremony site flowers
☐ Bride and Bridesmaid's bouquets
☐ Boutonnière's for Groom, Groomsmen, Ring Bearer and both Fathers
☐ Flowers for both the Bride and Groom's Mother
☐ Flowers to decorate the Flower Girl's basket and petals to toss
☐ Reception centerpieces and decorations
☐ Wedding cake, if applicable

Enter Flower Budget: _____

(Multiply total budget by 0.1)

Wedding Attire: 10%

This includes:

- ☐ Wedding dress
- ☐ Bride's headdress / veil
- ☐ Bride's lingerie
- ☐ Bride's jewelry
- ☐ Bride's shoes / wrap / gloves
- ☐ Hair and makeup
- ☐ Groom's tuxedo rental / shoes

Enter Wedding Attire Budget: _____

(Multiply total budget by 0.1)

Photography: 10%

This will include:

- ☐ Photography
- ☐ Videography
- ☐ Engagement photograph / portrait
- ☐ Wedding – album package
- ☐ Additional albums / photographs for gifts

Enter Photography Budget: _____

(Multiply total budget by 0.1)

Stationery: 4%

This includes:

- ☐ Invitations and enclosures (R.S.V.P. cards & envelopes, maps, etc.)
- ☐ Announcements

☐ Thank – you notes
☐ Postage
☐ Programs

Enter Stationery Budget: _____

(Multiply total budget by 0.04)

Miscellaneous: 6%

This is where all those random "little" items that add up so quickly to "real" money are placed. If the Bride and Groom will be covering the cost for most or all of these extra touches, they will need <u>more than</u> 6% of the total budget allocated here. In that case, they may need to become a little more frugal somewhere else.

☐ Bridesmaid's luncheon
☐ Attendant gifts
☐ Wedding gifts for each other
☐ Favors for the guests
☐ Welcome baskets for out-of-town guests
☐ Hotel room / "Honeymoon Suite" for the wedding night
☐ Wedding rings
☐ Rehearsal dinner
☐ Marriage license
☐ Church / Synagogue / ceremony venue fee
☐ Officiant's fee
☐ Assistant's fee

Enter Miscellaneous Budget: _____

(Multiply total budget by 0.06)

Chapter Nine

GENERAL TIPS & ADVICE:

This chapter list many cost saving tips and ideas to use while planning your wedding. Using these tips can save a substantial amount of money and time.

The Most Important Money Saving Tips

- You will save yourself an enormous amount of money if you get married during the off-season months of January, February, March and November.
- Getting married on any other day of the week other than Saturday.
- A common problem tend to happen to brides toward the end of planning:
    - 1st - around 3 months before your wedding, you'll begin to second-guess your decisions.
    - 2nd – You will get scared and think about what you can do to make your wedding better or more unique.
    - 3rd - Then you will ask friends, family, co-workers and anyone that will listen to you, about what they think of your new ideas.
    - 4th - and most dangerous…you make a few phone calls and start up-grading a few of your packages.

- The Solution - stick to your original budget. As the wedding draws near, trust your first instincts.
- Vendors are well aware of the disease. That's why every contract allows for you to upgrade a package at any time but there are rarely loopholes for downgrading.

The Wedding Attire Search

- If finances don't allow you to purchase a designer wedding dress, consider renting. Look at it this way, if you're the type who wouldn't even consider wearing your mother's dress, why do you need one collecting dust in the closet.
- Never mind buying an expensive silk gown. Stick to polyester blends. They're cheaper, don't wrinkle as much and are easier to clean.
- The more beading and detail on the gown, the more expensive.
- Most of the big bridal shops have huge sales once a year, usually held at hotels or other big venues.
- To take care of the something old-new-borrowed-blue, look to family and friends for items you can use.
- Go shopping for bridesmaids' dresses during prom season and after New Years. There's nothing written in stone that says you have to buy your bridesmaids dresses at a wedding shop, and generally your prices will be a bit cheaper elsewhere.
- Shop for those pretty little wedding shoes in the summer, when white shoes are on the shelves of every shoe and department store, or you'll have to buy them in a bridal shop and pay their prices. Shop in the afternoon, your feet swell during the day and they'll also be swollen on your wedding day. FB prime advice ... try "Payless".
- Men's Tuxedo rentals are pretty much all the same price no matter where you go. The thing to check on is the condition of the suits and accessories.

Flower Power

- Unless you plan on keeping your bouquet on display in your home, don't bother with a duplicate to toss.
- Instead of tossing your whole bouquet, just pick one flower to throw. We all know what condition the bride's bouquet is in after 30 women (or more) start clawing at it.
- Silk flowers save you a lot of money and they're already preserved. The Bride can have fresh flowers, but there really isn't any need for everyone else to go fresh.
- If you're using flowers in your centerpieces, decorations or large altar arrangements, go with silk. Would be nice if your guests could actually use the centerpieces that they just won again. You could re-use the decorations and larger arrangements at home, party accents or resell them on the Babbling Brides Board to another FB.

I Have No Idea How To Decorate!

- To decorate the head table and save money by buying vases, line them up and place the bouquets in them on the table and place votives in between.
- Before shopping for candles and candleholders anywhere else, be sure to check out a couple of dollar stores.
- Dollar stores and chains like Wal-Mart and Target also carry many items that can be used to decorate your ceremony or reception locations.
- When decorating the church or reception venue use silk flowers.
- Check with your florist or garden center to see if you can rent plants. Some florist allow rental of their items.
- Use your guest favors as your centerpieces. Buy a raised cake plate and display the favors on each table. Your MC can make an announcement explaining.

How Can I Cut Corners on the Invitations?

- To make your invitations more personal and less expensive, do them yourself. There are a number of paper stores and websites available where you can find original ideas and ways to make your own invitations.
- Order your invitations over the Internet instead of a printing shop (it's a little cheaper). Mail order is another possibility.
- Order a plain invitation from a company and decorate it yourself. All you need is a hole-puncher, ribbon and/or parchment paper.

I Don't Want to Spend a Fortune on Favors

- Please, go to a DOLLAR STORE first and check out their selection of party favors.
- Some stores decorate the gift for free and some don't, so make sure you ask.
- Instead of buying a trinket that will be tossed into a drawer, make a donation to a charity. This is a new trend that many brides are choosing. Pick a cause that means something to you. Your MC can say something like: "Instead of favors, the couple has decided to make a donation in their name to the Lung Cancer Society. The bride's grandfather passed 3 years ago from this disease." Donations always get a round of applause…ever see anyone clap for a candy dish?

Wedding Cakes too expensive? No Problem!

- Buying a cake made with different flavoured tiers will save you money as you wouldn't necessarily require a dessert table.
- To get away with not paying a cake cutting fee at your venue, purchase their sweet table but serve your wedding cake for dessert. This means you'll have to do your cake cutting as soon as your wedding party does their entrance. The staff will take the cake away and have it cut and plated in time for dessert.

- If you're having a dessert table, you really don't need to buy an elaborate wedding cake, try renting.
- Buy a plain wedding cake and decorate it yourself with silk or fresh flowers.

What about my Hair & Makeup?

- Try to hire one person or company that does both hair and makeup.
- Only the bride needs a trial.
- You can expect to pay anywhere from $40 to $100 for hair and $30 to $85 for makeup. Know that the more women you have that need these services, the cheaper the cost per person.
- If hair accessories are going to be put in anyone's hair, make sure you buy them yourself. If you leave this up to the hair stylist it'll cost more.
- If you have sensitive skin, we suggest that you do not go for a facial the week before your wedding. You don't want to be all broke out for the big day.
- Please get your nails done and make sure the groom's hands are also manicured. More than likely you'll be getting a picture that shows your hands and the wedding bands. People will be constantly asking to see your rings.
- Lastly, try to find a makeup and hair vendor that will do a trial a few months before the wedding. It gives you time to work out any areas you are not happy with and makes the wedding day process much quicker

Using a Caterer & choosing a Reception Venue

- Hire a caterer that supplies everything you need, plates, glassware, table cloths, etc.
- Make sure you're only charged for the services that you need. Some caterers have packages that include decorating and other items. If your venue is decorated already you won't need the

extras. Extras should be deducted from the bill or replaced with something else you want.

- Pick fruits and vegetables that are in season.
- Stick to serving food that everyone is familiar with. Fancy food is expensive.
- Buffets generally cost a good deal less and give your guests the opportunity to get up and mingle with the other guests, and they can pick exactly what they would like to eat.
- Make sure to read your contract and check to see if the gratuity is included. This goes for all services.
- Booking a venue that allows you to buy your own liquor is more work but saves you money.
- Depending on your culture and where you live in Canada, having a cash bar is totally acceptable. This can be a huge money saver.
- Consider only serving wine and domestic beers.
- Liquor (vodka, rum, rye, scotch) plus all the different mixes you'll need adds to your expenses.
- Liqueurs like Grand Marnier, Sambucca, etc. can put a real strain on the liquor budget.
- Do you really need that Champagne toast?
- Common sense tip - the more guests the more cash you're going to put out.
- Holding your reception in a hotel has a lot of good points. They usually decorate, have professional services, i.e. DJ, can cater well to large groups, and most likely will include the honeymoon suite, with discounted rooms for out-of-town guests.
- If you're having a wedding with 75 guests or under, consider having your reception at your favorite restaurant. You will already know the staff and how the food is.
- Order child meals for kids under 11.
- Order a teen meal (same as adults but no liquor) for ages 12 to 17.
- Your reception is the biggest expense. It's also where you can save the most money if you shop around and plan well!

Photographers charge too much!

Photographer's equipment and development costs alone are huge. Then there are batteries, film, an assistant and the hours of work on and after the wedding. You can save money on enlargements and albums but don't penny pinch when it comes to the photographer. After your wedding day, the only things you have left are your pictures and your video. These are the only 2 services that last a lifetime and can be passed down to the next generation.

- Biggest tip - hire a photographer that gives you your negatives, that way you can make as many copies of pictures from your wedding day as you want without having to order them from your photographer.
- If you choose a photographer that does not give you your negatives, always find out how long they keep your negatives on file and if you can obtain them when they are ready to discard them. Most photographers in general don't keep negatives past a couple of years. If your photographer still won't give you the negatives after that point without charging you money, I would question the ethics of the vendor.
- $1000.00 for a photographer is a great price but if they charge $40.00 for an 8 X 10, where's the savings. Don't just look at the photo packages or wedding day shoot costs; ask how much their enlargements are.
- If a package includes a couple's album and 2 parent albums, ask how much that same package would cost without any albums. Sometimes it's worth the savings to buy your own albums elsewhere and sometimes it's better to take the albums offered by your photographer.
- Unless you're doing a formal shoot at the bride or groom's house, you don't need a photographer there. Your wedding party and family will have their cameras out anyway.
- A great idea and one that many are using now is, putting a disposable camera on every table at the reception. Then you'll only need to book your photographer for the church, photo location and maybe to take a few detailed shots at the reception venue.

- You don't need your photographer to stay until 1am. Once the bouquet and garter tosses have taken place, there are no more major events to shoot. Your 1st & last dances look the same on film.

I think I'll just forget about a Video

Some couples think that having a video is a waste of money. How many times will we actually watch it? As necessary as still pictures are they cannot capture the mood, movement and sounds of your wedding day like a movie can. One of the biggest misconceptions is that you have a great memory and you'll remember everything about your day. You won't, you can't, there are too many things going on and you're on cloud 9. Keep this in mind.

- Go for packages with one camera coverage
- Pick a package with limited editing or none at all.
- If you can't afford a professional video, ask a friend or 2 that own their own video cameras to shoot the day for you. Putting an unfamiliar camera in someone else's hands is useless. Professionals know what to shoot and how to shoot it. So, give your friend a list of events that you want footage of and how you want each shot, for the entire day. Example:
  - Pre-Ceremony: Close-up footage for 10-seconds of the different decorations (altar arrangements, pew bows, wreath outside and unity candle)
  - The guys waiting. Ask the groom what he's thinking about.
  - The guests arriving (especially immediate family)

Do I Have To Pay a Fortune for Transportation?

- Shop around; there are so many limousine companies out there, prices do vary.

- There is no rule anywhere that says, "You have to have a stretch limousine." The smaller the car the cheaper.
- Other than the car and uniformed chauffeur, you really don't need any other extras.
- You can also save money by renting your vehicles from Budget, Hertz, etc. They all have new model luxury cars, sports cars and SUVs.
- You really don't need the limousine to take you home after the reception. Late-night pick-ups cost $100.00+
- Before the ceremony, have the limo pick up the bride and her bridesmaids. The groom, groomsmen and parents can take their own vehicles to the church. After the ceremony, the bride and groom can take the limo and the bridesmaids can hop in the groomsmen's cars.
- You may already know someone that owns a Cadillac or Lincoln, a fancy sports car or for fun a Beetle or an antique car. Give this person a call.
- Some couples need more than one limo. If this is the case for you, compare the cost of 2 to 3 limos vs. the cost of 1 limo bus or Chartered Bus.

Choosing Your Music Service

- Common sense, the least amount of people providing a service, the cheaper.
    - Ceremony - An organist is cheaper than a string duo, which is cheaper than a trio
    - Reception - A DJ is cheaper than a band
- The least amount of extras the cheaper. Lighting, smoke & bubble machines, other props, costumes, give-a ways, fireworks, the list is endless, all cost money. It's up to you.

A really expensive package doesn't mean that your party will last longer or that your non-dancing guests will feel the need to shake their booty for the first time in their life. But a crappy DJ or band will ruin your reception.

About the Author

Tiara Ward Cable is an event planner and owner of Create This! Event Planning & Management located in Sterling Heights, Michigan. She has a Bachelors of Arts Degree in Marketing from Michigan State University and a certification in event planning. Married with two energetic dogs, she enjoys traveling when she is not managing her business or planning events. Tiara Ward Cable has been in the Wedding & Event Planning industry for over six years and has planned countless weddings of all kinds. Please visit www.createthisevent.com for more about Create This! Event Planning & Management.

www.ingramcontent.com/pod-product-compliance
Lightning Source LLC
Chambersburg PA
CBHW062103280526
45788CB00003B/1336